Keto Blendtec Blender Cookbook for Beginners

1000-Day Low-Carb Ketogenic Diet Recipes for Total Health Rejuvenation, Weight Loss and Detox with Your Blendtec Blender

Paera Rodha

Table of contents

Introduction

Blendtec Blender on keto diet is very popular because it is very easy for people to follow this diet, moreover, it will short your time on cooking. With it you can enjoy the tasty recipes without gaining weight. With this Keto Blendtec Blender Cookbook for Beginners, you will cook better, tastier and faster keto meals for yourself and your family.

Save time with The Keto Blendtec Blender cookbook and get the food ready just in time for your family and friends. This book is suitable for both beginner and experienced cooks and has a wide variety of recipes for any taste. Using the recipes, you not only cook healthy, but you will also enjoy juicy meals that are perfectly cooked. With this book it will be easier than ever to make great tasting food that all the family will enjoy.

Chapter 1: Power Boosting Smoothie

Cinnamon Toast Smoothie

Preparation time: 5 minutes
Cooking time: 0 minute
Servings: 2

Ingredients:

- 1 ½ cup almond milk, unsweetened
- 1 ½ cup baby kale
- ½ teaspoon ground cinnamon
- 2 tablespoons almonds
- 1 banana, peeled
- 1 ½ tablespoon vanilla flavored protein powder
- ½ cup ice cubes

Method:

1. Plug in and switch on the NutriBullet blender and then add all the ingredients in the order into the jar.
2. Cover with the lid, press 'high', then press 'pulse' and let the ingredients blend until incorporated and smooth.
3. Divide smoothie between two glasses and then serve.

Nutrition Value:

- Calories: 312.7 Cal
- Fat: 13.8 g
- Carbs: 38 g
- Protein: 13.2 g
- Fiber: 9.3 g

Choco and Cherry Smoothie

Preparation time: 5 minutes
Cooking time: 0 minute
Servings: 2

Ingredients:

- 1 ½ cup almond milk, unsweetened
- 1 banana
- 1 cup collard greens
- ½ cup frozen cherries
- 2 tablespoons vanilla flavored protein powder
- 1 teaspoon cacao nibs

Method:

1. Plug in and switch on the NutriBullet blender and then add all the ingredients in the order into the jar.
2. Cover with the lid, press 'high', then press 'pulse' and let the ingredients blend until incorporated and smooth.
3. Divide smoothie between two glasses and then serve.

Nutrition Value:

- Calories: 285.9 Cal
- Fat: 6.5 g
- Carbs: 48.7 g
- Protein: 12.1 g
- Fiber: 7.9 g

Strawberry and Walnut Smoothie

Preparation time: 5 minutes

Cooking time: 0 minute

Servings: 2

Ingredients:

- 1 ½ cup almond milk, unsweetened
- 1 cup spinach
- 1 cup strawberries
- ¼ of avocado
- ½ teaspoon ground cinnamon
- 1 tablespoon walnuts
- 2 tablespoons vanilla protein powder
- 1 teaspoon flax seeds
- ½ cup ice cubes

Method:

1. Plug in and switch on the NutriBullet blender and then add all the ingredients in the order into the jar.
2. Cover with the lid, press 'high', then press 'pulse' and let the ingredients blend until incorporated and smooth.
3. Divide smoothie between two glasses and then serve.

Nutrition Value:

- Calories: 286.1 Cal
- Fat: 16.6 g
- Carbs: 26.3 g
- Protein: 13.5 g
- Fiber: 9.7 g

Cashew and Banana Smoothie

Preparation time: 5 minutes
Cooking time: 0 minute
Servings: 2

Ingredients:

- 1 ½ cup almond milk, unsweetened
- 1 cup spinach
- ¾ cup strawberries
- ½ of avocado
- 1 ¼ tablespoon cashew butter
- ½ of banana
- 2 tablespoons vanilla protein powder

Method:

1. Plug in and switch on the NutriBullet blender and then add all the ingredients in the order into the jar.
2. Cover with the lid, press 'high', then press 'pulse' and let the ingredients blend until incorporated and smooth.
3. Divide smoothie between two glasses and then serve.

Nutrition Value:

- Calories: 441.6 Cal
- Fat: 26.5 g
- Carbs: 42.7 g
- Protein: 16.5 g
- Fiber: 11.4 g

Apple and Peanut Butter Smoothie

Preparation time: 5 minutes

Cooking time: 0 minute

Servings: 2

Ingredients:

- 1 1/2 cup almond milk, unsweetened
- 1 cup kale
- 1 medium green apple, cored
- ½ of banana
- 1 teaspoon Maca powder
- 1 tablespoon vanilla flavored protein powder
- 1 tablespoon peanut butter, unsalted

Method:

1. Plug in and switch on the NutriBullet blender and then add all the ingredients in the order into the jar.
2. Cover with the lid, press 'high', then press 'pulse' and let the ingredients blend until incorporated and smooth.
3. Divide smoothie between two glasses and then serve.

Nutrition Value:

- Calories: 348.8 Cal
- Fat: 13.2 g
- Carbs: 49.6 g
- Protein: 10.7 g
- Fiber: 8.8 g

Avocado and Berry Smoothie

Preparation time: 5 minutes
Cooking time: 0 minute
Servings: 2

Ingredients:

- 2 cups almond milk, unsweetened
- ¼ cup mixed berries
- 1 cup mixed greens
- ¼ of avocado, pitted
- 1 teaspoon lime juice
- 1 tablespoon flaxseeds
- 3 tablespoons vanilla flavored protein powder
- 2/3 cup ice cubes

Method:

1. Plug in and switch on the NutriBullet blender and then add all the ingredients in the order into the jar.
2. Cover with the lid, press 'high', then press 'pulse' and let the ingredients blend until incorporated and smooth.
3. Divide smoothie between two glasses and then serve.

Nutrition Value:

- Calories: 295 Cal
- Fat: 17 g
- Carbs: 22.6 g
- Protein: 17.2 g
- Fiber: 9.4 g

Lemon Muffin Smoothie

Preparation time: 5 minutes
Cooking time: 0 minute
Servings: 2

Ingredients:

- 1 1/2 cup almond milk, unsweetened
- 1 cup spinach
- ½ of banana, peeled
- 1/4 cup oats, rolled
- 1/2 teaspoon lemon zest
- 1 tablespoon cashews, unsalted
- 1 teaspoon poppy seeds
- 1 tablespoon vanilla flavored protein powder
- 1 tablespoon lemon juice
- 1/2 teaspoon vanilla extract, unsweetened

Method:

1. Plug in and switch on the NutriBullet blender and then add all the ingredients in the order into the jar.
2. Cover with the lid, press 'high', then press 'pulse' and let the ingredients blend until incorporated and smooth.
3. Divide smoothie between two glasses and then serve.

Nutrition Value:

- Calories: 291.2 Cal
- Fat: 11 g
- Carbs: 39.4 g
- Protein: 11.4 g
- Fiber: 6.3 g

Strawberry Cupcake Smoothie

Preparation time: 5 minutes
Cooking time: 0 minute
Servings: 2

Ingredients:

- 1 ½ cup almond milk, unsweetened
- 2 tablespoons oats, rolled, gluten-free
- 1 1/2 cup spinach
- ½ of banana, peeled
- 1 cup strawberries, frozen
- 1 tablespoon chia seeds
- 2 tablespoons vanilla flavored protein powder

Method:

1. Plug in and switch on the NutriBullet blender and then add all the ingredients in the order into the jar.
2. Cover with the lid, press 'high', then press 'pulse' and let the ingredients blend until incorporated and smooth.
3. Divide smoothie between two glasses and then serve.

Nutrition Value:

- Calories: 320 Cal
- Fat: 10.5 g
- Carbs: 45.7 g
- Protein: 15 g
- Fiber: 45.7 g

Mango and Avocado Smoothie

Preparation time: 5 minutes

Cooking time: 0 minute

Servings: 2

Ingredients:

- 1 ½ cup coconut water
- 1 cup baby kale
- 1 cup frozen mango chunks
- ¼ of avocado
- 2 tablespoons vanilla flavored protein powder
- 1 tablespoon cashew

Method:

1. Plug in and switch on the NutriBullet blender and then add all the ingredients in the order into the jar.
2. Cover with the lid, press 'high', then press 'pulse' and let the ingredients blend until incorporated and smooth.
3. Divide smoothie between two glasses and then serve.

Nutrition Value:

- Calories: 327.6 Cal
- Fat: 11.7 g
- Carbs: 46.3 g
- Protein: 12.6 g
- Fiber: 6.5 g

Creamy Pineapple Smoothie

Preparation time: 5 minutes
Cooking time: 0 minute
Servings: 2

Ingredients:

- 1 ½ cup almond milk, unsweetened
- ¼ of medium avocado
- 1 ½ cup spinach
- 1 cup fresh pineapple chunks
- 1 ½ tablespoon vanilla flavored protein powder
- 1 teaspoon flaxseeds
- ½ cup ice cubes

Method:

1. Plug in and switch on the NutriBullet blender and then add all the ingredients in the order into the jar.
2. Cover with the lid, press 'high', then press 'pulse' and let the ingredients blend until incorporated and smooth.
3. Divide smoothie between two glasses and then serve.

Nutrition Value:

- Calories: 273 Cal
- Fat: 13 g
- Carbs: 32.5 g
- Protein: 10.9 g
- Fiber: 8.8 g

Chia Seeds and Coconut Smoothie

Preparation time: 5 minutes
Cooking time: 0 minute
Servings: 2

Ingredients:

- 1 ½ cup almond milk, unsweetened
- 1 cup spinach
- 1 teaspoon coconut butter
- 1 cup mixed berries, frozen
- 1 teaspoon ground turmeric
- 1 teaspoon chia seeds
- 2 1/2 teaspoon chocolate flavored Superfood Super boost

Method:

1. Plug in and switch on the NutriBullet blender and then add all the ingredients in the order into the jar.
2. Cover with the lid, press 'high', then press 'pulse' and let the ingredients blend until incorporated and smooth.
3. Divide smoothie between two glasses and then serve.

Nutrition Value:

- Calories: 228.1 Cal
- Fat: 9.9 g
- Carbs: 29.6 g
- Protein: 5 g
- Fiber: 10.7 g

Superfood Coffee Smoothie

Preparation time: 5 minutes
Cooking time: 0 minute
Servings: 2

Ingredients:

- 1/2 cup black coffee, cooled
- 1 cup almond milk, unsweetened
- 1 banana, peeled
- 5 strawberries, frozen
- 1 cup spinach
- 1/2 teaspoon ground cinnamon
- 1 tablespoon chocolate flavored Superfood Super boost
- 1 tablespoon coconut oil

Method:

1. Plug in and switch on the NutriBullet blender and then add all the ingredients in the order into the jar.
2. Cover with the lid, press 'high', then press 'pulse' and let the ingredients blend until incorporated and smooth.
3. Divide smoothie between two glasses and then serve.

Nutrition Value:

- Calories: 318.6 Cal
- Fat: 17.3 g
- Carbs: 40.5 g
- Protein: 4.7 g
- Fiber: 7.7 g

Chia, Mango and Berry Smoothie

Preparation time: 5 minutes
Cooking time: 0 minute
Servings: 2

Ingredients:

- 1 cup almond milk, unsweetened
- ½ cup Greek yogurt
- 1 cup frozen raspberries
- 1 cup frozen mango chunks
- 1 teaspoons honey
- 1 tablespoon chia seeds

Method:

1. Plug in and switch on the NutriBullet blender and then add all the ingredients in the order into the jar.
2. Cover with the lid, press 'high', then press 'pulse' and let the ingredients blend until incorporated and smooth.
3. Divide smoothie between two glasses and then serve.

Nutrition Value:

- Calories: 210 Cal
- Fat: 4 g
- Carbs: 32.2 g
- Protein: 9.1 g
- Fiber: 7.4 g

Caramel Apple Smoothie

Preparation time: 5 minutes
Cooking time: 0 minute
Servings: 2

Ingredients:

- ¾ cup almond milk, unsweetened
- 1 tablespoon almond butter, unsalted
- ½ of green apple
- 1 cup spinach
- 1 Medjool date, pitted
- 1 cup kale
- ¾ cup water
- 1/8 teaspoon ground cinnamon
- 2 tablespoons vanilla flavored protein powder
- 1/3 cup ice cubes

Method:

1. Plug in and switch on the NutriBullet blender and then add all the ingredients in the order into the jar.
2. Cover with the lid, press 'high', then press 'pulse' and let the ingredients blend until incorporated and smooth.
3. Divide smoothie between two glasses and then serve.

Nutrition Value:

- Calories: 311.4 Cal
- Fat: 13.2 g
- Carbs: 38.6 g
- Protein: 14 g
- Fiber: 8.6 g

Banana Cherry Powder Smoothie

Preparation time: 5 minutes
Cooking time: 0 minute
Servings: 2

Ingredients:

- 2 cups almond milk, unsweetened
- 2 bananas, peeled
- 2/3 cup frozen cherries
- 2 tablespoons vanilla flavored protein powder

Method:

1. Plug in and switch on the NutriBullet blender and then add all the ingredients in the order into the jar.
2. Cover with the lid, press 'high', then press 'pulse' and let the ingredients blend until incorporated and smooth.
3. Divide smoothie between two glasses and then serve.

Nutrition Value:

- Calories: 258 Cal
- Fat: 5.4 g
- Carbs: 45.4 g
- Protein: 11 g
- Fiber: 6 g

Green Tea and Mixed Fruits Smoothie

Preparation time: 5 minutes
Cooking time: 0 minute
Servings: 2

Ingredients:

- 1 ½ cup green tea
- 2 plums, pitted, halved
- 2 peaches, pitted, quartered
- 2 nectarines, pitted, quartered
- 2 limes, juiced

Method:

1. Plug in and switch on the NutriBullet blender and then add all the ingredients in the order into the jar.
2. Cover with the lid, press 'high', then press 'pulse' and let the ingredients blend until incorporated and smooth.
3. Divide smoothie between two glasses and then serve.

Nutrition Value:

- Calories: 181 Cal
- Fat: 1.2 g
- Carbs: 37.2 g
- Protein: 3.5 g
- Fiber: 7.5 g

Blackberries Smoothie

Preparation time: 5 minutes
Cooking time: 0 minute
Servings: 2

Ingredients:

- 1 cup almond milk, unsweetened
- ½ cup water
- 1 tablespoon almond butter, unsalted
- ½ cup frozen blackberries
- 2 cups spinach
- ½ cup frozen cherries
- ½ tablespoon grated ginger
- 1 teaspoon ground cinnamon
- 2 tablespoons vanilla flavored protein powder
- ½ tablespoon coconut oil

Method:

1. Plug in and switch on the NutriBullet blender and then add all the ingredients in the order into the jar.
2. Cover with the lid, press 'high', then press 'pulse' and let the ingredients blend until incorporated and smooth.
3. Divide smoothie between two glasses and then serve.

Nutrition Value:

- Calories: 371.5 Cal
- Fat: 20.8 g
- Carbs: 35.7 g
- Protein: 15.4 g
- Fiber: 11.4 g

Carrot Cake Smoothie

Preparation time: 5 minutes
Cooking time: 0 minute
Servings: 2

Ingredients:

- 1 ½ cup almond milk, unsweetened
- ¼ cup Greek yogurt, plain, non-fat
- 1/2 cup diced carrot
- 2 Medjool dates, pitted
- 1/4 teaspoon ground cinnamon
- 1 tablespoon coconut flakes, unsweetened
- 1/8 teaspoon ground nutmeg

Method:

1. Plug in and switch on the NutriBullet blender and then add all the ingredients in the order into the jar.
2. Cover with the lid, press 'high', then press 'pulse' and let the ingredients blend until incorporated and smooth.
3. Divide smoothie between two glasses and then serve.

Nutrition Value:

- Calories: 301.1 Cal
- Fat: 8.7 g
- Carbs: 51.7 g
- Protein: 10 g
- Fiber: 7.1 g

Chapter 2: High – Protein Smoothie

Spinach and Banana Protein Smoothie

Preparation time: 5 minutes
Cooking time: 0 minute
Servings: 2

Ingredients:

- 1 1/2 cup almond milk, unsweetened
- ½ of banana
- 2 tablespoons Greek yogurt
- 1 cup spinach
- 1 cup mixed berries, frozen
- 1/2 teaspoon ground cinnamon
- 2 tablespoons vanilla flavored protein powder
- 1 tablespoon almond butter, no added salt

Method:

1. Plug in and switch on the NutriBullet blender and then add all the ingredients in the order into the jar.
2. Cover with the lid, press 'high', then press 'pulse' and let the ingredients blend until incorporated and smooth.
3. Divide smoothie between two glasses and then serve.

Nutrition Value:

- Calories: 367 Cal
- Fat: 14.8 g
- Carbs: 44.1 g
- Protein: 18.2 g
- Fiber: 11.1 g

Carrot Protein Shake

Preparation time: 5 minutes

Cooking time: 0 minute

Servings: 2

Ingredients:

- 1 1/2 cup almond milk, unsweetened
- 1 cup spinach
- ½ of frozen banana, peeled
- 1 cup baby carrots
- 1 tablespoons raisin, seedless
- 1/8 teaspoon ground nutmeg
- 2 tablespoons vanilla flavored protein powder
- 1/8 teaspoon ground clove
- 1/2 teaspoon ground cinnamon
- 1/3 cup ice cubes

Method:

1. Plug in and switch on the NutriBullet blender and then add all the ingredients in the order into the jar.
2. Cover with the lid, press 'high', then press 'pulse' and let the ingredients blend until incorporated and smooth.
3. Divide shake between two glasses and then serve.

Nutrition Value:

- Calories: 240 Cal
- Fat: 6.7 g
- Carbs: 36.2 g
- Protein: 11.8 g
- Fiber: 8.8 g

Pumpkin Pie Protein Smoothie

Preparation time: 5 minutes

Cooking time: 0 minute

Servings: 2

Ingredients:

- 1 1/2 cup almond milk, unsweetened
- ½ of banana
- 1/4 cup pumpkin puree
- 1/2 cup peach, pitted
- 1/2 teaspoon ground cinnamon
- 1/2 cup fresh pineapple chunks
- 1/2 teaspoon ground allspice
- 1 tablespoon vanilla flavored protein powder

Method:

1. Plug in and switch on the NutriBullet blender and then add all the ingredients in the order into the jar.
2. Cover with the lid, press 'high', then press 'pulse' and let the ingredients blend until incorporated and smooth.
3. Divide smoothie between two glasses and then serve.

Nutrition Value:

- Calories: 230.8 Cal
- Fat: 5.1 g
- Carbs: 43.9 g
- Protein: 8.2 g
- Fiber: 8.3 g

Green Protein Smoothie

Preparation time: 5 minutes
Cooking time: 0 minute
Servings: 2

Ingredients:

- 1 1/2 cup almond milk, unsweetened
- ½ of banana, peeled
- 1/2 cup Greek yogurt
- 2 cups spinach
- 1 tablespoon peanut butter, unsalted
- 1/2 teaspoon ground cinnamon
- 1 tablespoon vanilla flavored protein powder

Method:

1. Plug in and switch on the NutriBullet blender and then add all the ingredients in the order into the jar.
2. Cover with the lid, press 'high', then press 'pulse' and let the ingredients blend until incorporated and smooth.
3. Divide smoothie between two glasses and then serve.

Nutrition Value:

- Calories: 322.7 Cal
- Fat: 13.4 g
- Carbs: 31 g
- Protein: 24.5 g
- Fiber: 5.4 g

Zucchini, Avocado and Almond Smoothie

Preparation time: 5 minutes
Cooking time: 0 minute
Servings: 2

Ingredients:

- 1 1/2 cup almond milk, unsweetened
- 1 tablespoon almond butter
- ½ of banana
- 1/2 cup fresh zucchini
- 1 teaspoon cacao nibs
- ½ of avocado
- 1/2 tablespoon cacao powder
- 2 tablespoons vanilla flavored protein powder
- 2/3 cup ice cubes

Method:

1. Plug in and switch on the NutriBullet blender and then add all the ingredients in the order into the jar.
2. Cover with the lid, press 'high', then press 'pulse' and let the ingredients blend until incorporated and smooth.
3. Divide smoothie between two glasses and then serve.

Nutrition Value:

- Calories: 419.3 Cal
- Fat: 26.5 g
- Carbs: 35.4 g
- Protein: 16.3 g
- Fiber: 12 g

Muesli Smoothie

Preparation time: 5 minutes
Cooking time: 0 minute
Servings: 2

Ingredients:

- 1 cup almond milk, unsweetened
- 1 medium green apple, cored
- 1/2 cup rolled oats
- 1 banana, peeled
- 1 teaspoon ground cinnamon
- ¼ cup roasted pecans, unsalted
- 2 tablespoons vanilla flavored protein powder

Method:

1. Plug in and switch on the NutriBullet blender and then add all the ingredients in the order into the jar.
2. Cover with the lid, press 'high', then press 'pulse' and let the ingredients blend until incorporated and smooth.
3. Divide smoothie between two glasses and then serve.

Nutrition Value:

- Calories: 675.1 Cal
- Fat: 23.5 g
- Carbs: 97.4 g
- Protein: 25.8 g
- Fiber: 16.3 g

Strawberry Protein Punch

Preparation time: 5 minutes
Cooking time: 0 minute
Servings: 2

Ingredients:

- 1/2 cup almond milk, unsweetened
- 2 cups kale
- 1 cup water
- 1 cup frozen strawberries
- 1 1/2 tablespoon cashew butter, unsalted
- 1/2 cup frozen cherries
- 1 tablespoon rolled oats, rolled, gluten-free
- 1/4 teaspoon vanilla extract, unsweetened
- 2 tablespoons vanilla flavored protein powder

Method:

1. Plug in and switch on the NutriBullet blender and then add all the ingredients in the order into the jar.
2. Cover with the lid, press 'high', then press 'pulse' and let the ingredients blend until incorporated and smooth.
3. Divide smoothie between two glasses and then serve.

Nutrition Value:

- Calories: 346.1 Cal
- Fat: 16 g
- Carbs: 40 g
- Protein: 15.2 g
- Fiber: 8.2 g

Grape Protein Smoothie

Preparation time: 5 minutes
Cooking time: 0 minute
Servings: 2

Ingredients:

- 3 cups almond milk, unsweetened
- 1 banana, peeled
- 2 cups spinach
- 4 tablespoons orange juice
- 2 cups grapes
- 2 tablespoons dried goji berries
- 2 tablespoons vanilla flavored protein powder
- ½ cup frozen green peas

Method:

1. Plug in and switch on the NutriBullet blender and then add all the ingredients in the order into the jar.
2. Cover with the lid, press 'high', then press 'pulse' and let the ingredients blend until incorporated and smooth.
3. Divide smoothie between two glasses and then serve.

Nutrition Value:

- Calories: 304.2 Cal
- Fat: 5 g
- Carbs: 60.1 g
- Protein: 10.7 g
- Fiber: 7 g

Blackberry and Almond Shake

Preparation time: 5 minutes
Cooking time: 0 minute
Servings: 2

Ingredients:

- 1/2 cup coconut milk, canned
- 1 cup water
- 1/2 cup blackberries, frozen
- 2 tablespoons macadamia nuts
- 1 teaspoon hemp seeds
- 1 packet of liquid stevia
- 1/8 teaspoon sea salt
- 1 1/2 tablespoon vanilla flavored protein powder
- 1 teaspoon MCT oil
- 2/3 cup ice cubes

Method:

1. Plug in and switch on the NutriBullet blender and then add all the ingredients in the order into the jar.
2. Cover with the lid, press 'high', then press 'pulse' and let the ingredients blend until incorporated and smooth.
3. Divide smoothie between two glasses and then serve.

Nutrition Value:

- Calories: 490.9 Cal
- Fat: 44.3 g
- Carbs: 19.6 g
- Protein: 11.4 g
- Fiber: 6 g

Pumpkin Spice Protein Smoothie

Preparation time: 5 minutes

Cooking time: 0 minute

Servings: 2

Ingredients:

- 1 1/2 cup almond milk, unsweetened
- 1/3 cup pumpkin puree
- 1 tablespoon almond butter, unsalted
- 1 banana, peeled
- 1/4 teaspoon pumpkin spice
- 2 tablespoons vanilla flavored protein powder
- 1/2 cup ice cubes

Method:

1. Plug in and switch on the NutriBullet blender and then add all the ingredients in the order into the jar.
2. Cover with the lid, press 'high', then press 'pulse' and let the ingredients blend until incorporated and smooth.
3. Divide smoothie between two glasses and then serve.

Nutrition Value:

- Calories: 346.8 Cal
- Fat: 15.7 g
- Carbs: 42 g
- Protein: 15.3 g
- Fiber: 10.3 g

Chapter 3: Green Smoothie

Blueberry Yogurt Smoothie

Preparation time: 5 minutes

Cooking time: 0 minute

Servings: 2

Ingredients:

- 1 1/2 cup almond milk, unsweetened
- 1 cup blueberries
- 1/2 cup Greek yogurt
- 1 cup kale
- 1/2 tablespoon grated ginger
- 1 tablespoon lemon juice
- 1 tablespoon SuperFood Super Boost

Method:

1. Plug in and switch on the NutriBullet blender and then add all the ingredients in the order into the jar.
2. Cover with the lid, press 'high', then press 'pulse' and let the ingredients blend until incorporated and smooth.
3. Divide smoothie between two glasses and then serve.

Nutrition Value:

- Calories: 259.6 Cal
- Fat: 5.3 g
- Carbs: 39.7 g
- Protein: 17.1 g
- Fiber: 6.7 g

Apple and Tofu Smoothie

Preparation time: 5 minutes
Cooking time: 0 minute
Servings: 2

Ingredients:

- 1 cup almond milk, unsweetened
- 2 cups Swiss chard
- ½ cup coconut water
- 1 medium red apple, cored
- ½ cup tofu, firm
- 2 tablespoons rolled oats
- 1 tablespoon almond butter, unsalted
- ½ teaspoon ground cinnamon
- 2 tablespoons vanilla flavored protein powder

Method:

1. Plug in and switch on the NutriBullet blender and then add all the ingredients in the order into the jar.
2. Cover with the lid, press 'high', then press 'pulse' and let the ingredients blend until incorporated and smooth.
3. Divide smoothie between two glasses and then serve.

Nutrition Value:

- Calories: 444.1 Cal
- Fat: 17.7 g
- Carbs: 51.5 g
- Protein: 22.7 g
- Fiber: 11.3 g

Chia and Zucchini Smoothie

Preparation time: 5 minutes
Cooking time: 0 minute
Servings: 2

Ingredients:

- 1 ½ cup almond milk, unsweetened
- 1 cup zucchini, fresh
- 1 tablespoon almond butter, unsalted
- 1 tablespoon chia seeds
- 1 teaspoon turmeric powder
- 1/4 teaspoon ground cinnamon
- 3 tablespoons vanilla flavored protein powder
- 2/3 cup ice cubes

Method:

1. Plug in and switch on the NutriBullet blender and then add all the ingredients in the order into the jar.
2. Cover with the lid, press 'high', then press 'pulse' and let the ingredients blend until incorporated and smooth.
3. Divide smoothie between two glasses and then serve.

Nutrition Value:

- Calories: 306.5 Cal
- Fat: 18.3 g
- Carbs: 20.4 g
- Protein: 19.6 g
- Fiber: 8.6 g

Herbal Smoothie

Preparation time: 5 minutes
Cooking time: 0 minute
Servings: 2

Ingredients:

- 1 1/2 cup water
- 3 cups Swiss Chard
- ¾ cup frozen blueberries
- 1 tablespoon cilantro leaves
- 1/4 cup roasted cashews, unsalted
- 1 tablespoon mint leaves
- 2 teaspoons superfood essential greens
- ½ tablespoon lime juice

Method:

1. Plug in and switch on the NutriBullet blender and then add all the ingredients in the order into the jar.
2. Cover with the lid, press 'high', then press 'pulse' and let the ingredients blend until incorporated and smooth.
3. Divide smoothie between two glasses and then serve.

Nutrition Value:

- Calories: 292.6 Cal
- Fat: 17 g
- Carbs: 33.5 g
- Protein: 7.8 g
- Fiber: 7.4 g

Tropic Smoothie

Preparation time: 5 minutes
Cooking time: 0 minute
Servings: 2

Ingredients:

- 1 cup coconut water
- ¼ of medium cucumber
- ½ cup fresh pineapple chunks
- 1 cup spinach
- 5 mint leaves
- 1 tablespoon chia seeds
- ½ tablespoon lime juice
- 1 tablespoon vanilla flavored protein powder

Method:

1. Plug in and switch on the NutriBullet blender and then add all the ingredients in the order into the jar.
2. Cover with the lid, press 'high', then press 'pulse' and let the ingredients blend until incorporated and smooth.
3. Divide smoothie between two glasses and then serve.

Nutrition Value:

- Calories: 180.1 Cal
- Fat: 4.3 g
- Carbs: 30.6 g
- Protein: 7.8 g
- Fiber: 6.1 g

Skinny Green Smoothie

Preparation time: 5 minutes
Cooking time: 0 minute
Servings: 2

Ingredients:

- 1 cup almond milk, unsweetened
- 1 cup spinach
- ½ of medium cucumber
- ½ cup coconut water
- ½ cup parsley
- 1 medium green apple, cored
- 1 tablespoon coconut oil
- 5 mint leaves
- 1 tablespoon SuperFood Super Boost

Method:

1. Plug in and switch on the NutriBullet blender and then add all the ingredients in the order into the jar.
2. Cover with the lid, press 'high', then press 'pulse' and let the ingredients blend until incorporated and smooth.
3. Divide smoothie between two glasses and then serve.

Nutrition Value:

- Calories: 343.2 Cal
- Fat: 17.1 g
- Carbs: 44.5 g
- Protein: 5.2 g
- Fiber: 9 g

Banana Kale Smoothie

Preparation time: 5 minutes

Cooking time: 0 minute

Servings: 2

Ingredients:

- 1 1/2 cup water
- 1 banana, peeled
- 1 cup kale
- 1/2 cup frozen mixed berries
- 1 tablespoon hemp seeds
- 2 teaspoons SuperFood Super Boost

Method:

1. Plug in and switch on the NutriBullet blender and then add all the ingredients in the order into the jar.
2. Cover with the lid, press 'high', then press 'pulse' and let the ingredients blend until incorporated and smooth.
3. Divide smoothie between two glasses and then serve.

Nutrition Value:

- Calories: 228.5 Cal
- Fat: 6.1 g
- Carbs: 41.6 g
- Protein: 6 g
- Fiber: 7.8 g

Citrus Smoothie

Preparation time: 5 minutes
Cooking time: 0 minute
Servings: 2

Ingredients:

- 1 cup coconut water
- 2 cups kale
- ½ cup water
- ¼ cup cucumber pieces
- 1 orange
- 1 tablespoon lemon juice
- 1 teaspoon honey
- 1 teaspoon superfood essential greens

Method:

1. Plug in and switch on the NutriBullet blender and then add all the ingredients in the order into the jar.
2. Cover with the lid, press 'high', then press 'pulse' and let the ingredients blend until incorporated and smooth.
3. Divide smoothie between two glasses and then serve.

Nutrition Value:

- Calories: 152 Cal
- Fat: 0.7 g
- Carbs: 36.6 g
- Protein: 3 g
- Fiber: 5.3 g

Chapter 4: Meals

Pumpkin Cream Soup

Preparation time: 5 minutes
Cooking time: 15 minutes
Servings: 4

Ingredients:

- ½ of medium white onion, peeled, sliced
- 1 ½ cup canned chickpeas
- 1 tablespoon minced garlic
- 1 teaspoon grated ginger
- ½ teaspoon sea salt
- 1/8 teaspoon ground nutmeg
- ¼ teaspoon ground black pepper
- 1/8 teaspoon ground clove
- 1 tablespoon unsalted butter
- 1 tablespoon olive oil
- 2 cups vegetable broth
- 2 cups pumpkin puree
- ½ cup heavy cream

Method:

1. Take a medium pot, place it over medium heat, add oil and butter and when butter melts, add onion, chickpeas and garlic, stir and cook for 3 to 4 minutes until softened.
2. Then add all the spices, stir until mixed, then remove pot from heat and let it cool for 10 minutes.
3. Transfer chickpeas mixture into the NutriBullet blender and then add remaining ingredients into the jar except for cream.
4. Plug in and switch on the blender, cover with the lid, and then press 'high', then press 'pulse' for 30 until smooth mixture comes together.

5. Pour the soup into the pot, stir in cream until well combined, return pot over medium heat and let the soup simmer for 10 minutes until thick and hot.
6. When done, ladle soup into bowls and then serve.

Nutrition Value:

- Calories: 292 Cal
- Fat: 19.1 g
- Carbs: 26.3 g
- Protein: 7.2 g
- Fiber: 9 g

Broccoli Cheese Soup

Preparation time: 5 minutes
Cooking time: 15 minutes
Servings: 2

Ingredients:

- 3 cups broccoli florets, chopped
- 2 cups almond milk, unsweetened
- 2 teaspoons diced white onion
- 1 cup shredded cheddar cheese, low-fat
- 1 bouillon cube

Method:

1. Take a large heatproof bowl, place broccoli florets in it, cover with a plastic wrap and then microwave for 5 to 8 minutes until tender.
2. Drain the broccoli, transfer them into the NutriBullet blender and then add remaining ingredients.
3. Plug in and switch on the blender, cover with the lid, press 'high', then press 'pulse' for 1 minute until smooth.
4. Pour the soup into the pot, place pot over medium heat and let the soup simmer for 10 minutes until thick and hot.
5. When done, ladle soup into bowls and then serve.

Nutrition Value:

- Calories: 130 Cal
- Fat: 2.5 g
- Carbs: 15 g
- Protein: 14 g
- Fiber: 4 g

Cauliflower Mac and Cheese

Preparation time: 10 minutes
Cooking time: 15 minutes
Servings: 5

Ingredients:

- ¼ cup cauliflower florets, chopped
- 1 ½ cup macaroni noodles, cooked
- 1 cup shredded cheddar cheese
- 2 tablespoons unsalted butter, softened
- ¼ cup ricotta cheese
- 2 tablespoons whole milk

Method:

1. Take a large heatproof bowl, place cauliflower florets in it, cover with a plastic wrap and then microwave for 5 to 8 minutes until tender.
2. Drain the cauliflower, let it cool for 15 minutes, then transfer into the NutriBullet blender and pour in milk.
3. Plug in and switch on the NutriBullet blender, cover with the lid, press 'high', then press 'pulse' until smoot, then add cheeses and butter and pulse again until blended.
4. Pour the sauce into the pot, place pot over medium heat and simmer for 5 minutes until hot.
5. Add cooked macaroni into the pot, toss until coated and continue cooking for 2 minutes until thoroughly warm.
6. Serve straight away.

Nutrition Value:

- Calories: 292.3 Cal
- Fat: 14.2 g
- Carbs: 29.2 g
- Protein: 11.7 g
- Fiber: 1.3 g

Pumpkin and Beet Soup

Preparation time: 10 minutes
Cooking time: 45 minutes
Servings: 2

Ingredients:

- 2 medium beets, peeled, chopped
- ¼ of a medium white onion, peeled, chopped
- 3 ½ small red potatoes, peeled, chopped
- ½ teaspoon ground cinnamon
- ¼ teaspoon sea salt
- ¼ teaspoon ground nutmeg
- ¼ teaspoon ground black pepper
- 2 teaspoons olive oil
- 1 cup pumpkin puree
- 2 tablespoons pumpkin seeds, unsalted
- ½ cup coconut milk, unsweetened
- 1 ½ cup water

Method:

1. Switch on the oven, then set it to 400 degrees F and let it preheat.
2. Then take a baking tray, line it with foil, spread onion, potatoes and beet pieces on it, season with salt and drizzle with oil.
3. Toss well until all the vegetables are coated with oil and salt and then bake for 35 minutes until softened.
4. When done, let the vegetables cool for 15 to 20 minutes and then transfer then into the NutriBullet blender.
5. Plug in and switch on the blender, add remaining ingredients into the jar, cover with the lid, press 'high', then press 'pulse' for 40 to 50 seconds until smooth.
6. Pour the soup into the pot, place pot over medium heat and let the soup simmer for 10 minutes until thick and hot.
7. When done, ladle soup into bowls and then serve.

Nutrition Value:

- Calories: 386.9 Cal
- Fat: 10.5 g
- Carbs: 67.7 g

- Protein: 11.4 g
- Fiber: 13.8 g

Potato Pancakes

Preparation time: 5 minutes
Cooking time: 8 minutes
Servings: 4

Ingredients:

- 1 small white onion, peeled, halved
- 2 eggs, room temperature
- 2 tablespoons all-purpose flour
- 1/8 teaspoon cayenne pepper
- ½ teaspoon salt
- 2 medium potatoes, peeled, 1-inch cubed
- 2 tablespoons olive oil

Method:

1. Plug in and switch on the NutriBullet blender and then add onion and eggs into the jar.
2. Cover with the lid, press 'high', press 'pulse' until blended, then add potatoes and continue processing until chopped.
3. Tip the mixture into a medium bowl, add flour in it and then stir in salt and cayenne pepper until well combined.
4. Take a medium skillet pan, add 2 tablespoons oil in it and when hot, drop pancake batter into it.
5. Spread the batter evenly to shape pancake and then fry for 2 to 3 minutes per side until golden brown and cooked.
6. Transfer pancakes to a plate lined with paper towels and then serve.

Nutrition Value:

- Calories: 263 Cal
- Fat: 17 g
- Carbs: 23 g
- Protein: 6 g
- Fiber: 3 g

Overnight Oats

Preparation time: 5 minutes
Cooking time: 0 minute
Servings: 6

Ingredients:

- 5 cups almond milk, unsweetened
- 2 cups coconut water
- 3 cups rolled oats
- ¼ cup chia seeds
- 1 cup Greek yogurt
- 2 cups strawberries
- 2 tablespoons ground cinnamon
- 2 tablespoons agave nectar
- 2 tablespoons vanilla extract, unsweetened

Method:

1. Take a large bowl, pour in milk and water, add oats and chia seeds and stir until combined.
2. Plug in and switch on the NutriBullet blender and then add remaining ingredients in the order into the jar.
3. Cover with the lid, press 'high', then press 'pulse' and let the ingredients blend until incorporated and smooth.
4. Transfer the blended mixture into the bowl containing oats mixture, stir until combined, cover the bowl with its lid and refrigerate for a minimum of 8 hours.
5. When done, distribute oats evenly among bowls, garnish with favorite toppings and then serve.

Nutrition Value:

- Calories: 312.8 Cal
- Fat: 7.1 g
- Carbs: 49.5 g
- Protein: 12.3 g
- Fiber: 9.3 g

Cookie Dough

Preparation time: 10 minutes
Cooking time: 0 minute
Servings: 12

Ingredients:

- 15 ounces canned chickpeas
- 2 tablespoons almond milk
- ¼ teaspoon salt
- 3 tablespoons coconut sugar
- 1 teaspoon vanilla extract, unsweetened
- 1 tablespoon maple syrup
- ¼ cup sunflower seed butter, unsweetened
- ¼ cup mini chocolate chips

Method:

1. Plug in and switch on the NutriBullet blender and then add all the ingredients in the order into the jar except for chocolate chips.
2. Cover with the lid, press 'high', then press 'pulse' and let the ingredients blend until incorporated and smooth.
3. Transfer the mixture into a freezer proof bowl, fold in chocolate chips, then cover with a lid and let it freeze for a minimum of 15 minutes until thoroughly chilled.
4. When ready to eat, spoon dough into a bowl and then serve it with favorite toping.

Nutrition Value:

- Calories: 93 Cal
- Fat: 4 g
- Carbs: 11 g
- Protein: 3 g
- Fiber: 2 g

Strawberry and Watermelon Slush

Preparation time: 5 minutes
Cooking time: 0 minute
Servings: 4

Ingredients:

- 2 cups seedless watermelon chunks
- 1/3 cup lemon juice
- 2 cups fresh strawberries, halved
- 1/3 cup coconut sugar
- 2 cups ice cubes

Method:

1. Plug in and switch on the NutriBullet blender and then add all the ingredients in the order into the jar except for ice cubes.
2. Cover with the lid, press 'high', then press 'pulse' and let the ingredients blend until incorporated and smooth.
3. Add ice cubes into the jar, cover with the lid and then pulse until slushy.
4. Divide slush between four bowls and then serve.

Nutrition Value:

- Calories: 112 Cal
- Fat: 0 g
- Carbs: 30 g
- Protein: 1 g
- Fiber: 2 g

Strawberry and Almond Dessert Smoothie

Preparation time: 5 minutes
Cooking time: 0 minute
Servings: 2

Ingredients:

- 3 cups almond milk, unsweetened
- 2 frozen bananas
- ½ cup almonds
- 3 cups fresh strawberries
- 10 mint leaves
- 1 teaspoon ground cinnamon
- 2 tablespoons chia seeds
- 2 tablespoons vanilla flavored protein powder
- 2 tablespoons coconut oil

Method:

1. Plug in and switch on the NutriBullet blender and then add all the ingredients in the order into the jar.
2. Cover with the lid, press 'high', then press 'pulse' and let the ingredients blend until incorporated and smooth.
3. Divide smoothie between two glasses and then serve.

Nutrition Value:

- Calories: 594.4 Cal
- Fat: 37 g
- Carbs: 57.8 g
- Protein: 15.7 g
- Fiber: 16.4 g

Sweet Potato Pie

Preparation time: 10 minutes
Cooking time: 60 minutes
Servings: 8

Ingredients:

For the Crust:

- 1 cup unroasted pecans and more for topping
- 1 cup unsalted walnuts and more for topping
- 1 cup Medjool dates, pitted

For the Filling:

- 1 cup coconut milk, unsweetened
- 2 sweet potato, roasted, cooled, peeled
- 1 tablespoon vanilla extract, unsweetened
- 1 teaspoon maple syrup
- 1/8 teaspoon sea salt
- ½ teaspoon ground cinnamon

Method:

1. Switch on the oven, then set it to 350 degrees F and let it preheat.
2. Prepare the crust and for this, plug in and switch on the NutriBullet blender and then add pecans and nuts into the jar.
3. Cover with the lid, press 'high', press 'pulse' until ingredients have crumbled and then transfer the nut mixture into a small bowl.
4. Add dates into the blender jar, cover with the lid, press 'high', press 'pulse' until dates are broken and then transfer into the bowl containing nuts mixture and stir until combined.
5. Take a springform pan, place nuts-dates mixture in it and then spread it evenly in the bottom of the pan, pressing firmly.

6. Prepare the filling and for this, place all of its ingredients into the jar of the NutriBullet blender, cover with the lid, press 'high', and then press 'pulse' until smooth.
7. Pour the filling into the prepared crust and then bake into the heated oven for 1 hour until set.
8. When done, top the pie with walnuts and pecans and serve its slice with a dollop of whipped cream.

Nutrition Value:

- Calories: 294.5 Cal
- Fat: 19.1 g
- Carbs: 30.2 g
- Protein: 4.7 g
- Fiber: 5.4 g

Brownie-tini

Preparation time: 5 minutes
Cooking time: 0 minute
Servings: 4

Ingredients:

- 1 cup vodka
- 1 cup half-and-half
- 1 cup crumbled baked brownies
- ½ cup Irish cream liqueur
- ½ cup ice cubes
- Grated chocolate, as needed for garnish

Method:

1. Plug in and switch on the NutriBullet blender and then add all the ingredients in the order into the jar, except for chocolate.
2. Cover with the lid, press 'high', then press 'pulse' and let the ingredients blend until incorporated and smooth.
3. Divide martini evenly among four chilled glasses, top with grated chocolate and then serve.

Nutrition Value:

- Calories: 353 Cal
- Fat: 20.8 g
- Carbs: 35.3 g
- Protein: 6.2 g
- Fiber: 3.2 g

Pumpkin Cheesecake

Preparation time: 10 minutes
Cooking time: 0 minute
Servings: 8

Ingredients:

For the Crust:

- 1 cup unroasted pecans and more for topping
- 1 cup unsalted walnuts and more for topping
- 1 cup Medjool dates, pitted

For the Filling:

- ½ cup coconut milk, unsweetened
- ½ cup pumpkin puree
- 2 cups cashews, soaked in hot water for 1 hour
- 1/8 teaspoon sea salt
- ¼ teaspoon ground cinnamon
- 2 tablespoons lemon juice
- ¼ teaspoon pumpkin spice
- ½ cup maple syrup
- 1 teaspoon vanilla extract, unsweetened
- 3 tablespoons coconut oil

Method:

1. Prepare the crust and for this, plug in and switch on the NutriBullet blender and then add pecans and nuts into the jar.
2. Cover with the lid, press 'high', press 'pulse' until ingredients have crumbled and then transfer the nut mixture into a small bowl.
3. Add dates into the blender jar, cover with the lid, press 'high', press 'pulse' until dates are broken and then transfer into the bowl containing nuts mixture and stir until combined.

4. Take a springform pan, place nuts-dates mixture in it and then spread it evenly in the bottom of the pan, pressing firmly.
5. Prepare the filling and for this, drain the cashews, add then into the jar of the NutriBullet blender along with remaining ingredients, cover with the lid, press 'high', and then press 'pulse' until smooth.
6. Pour the filling into the prepared crust, spread it evenly, smooth the top by using a spatula and let it freeze for a minimum of 4 hours until pie is set.
7. When done, top the pie with walnuts and pecans and serve its slice with a dollop of whipped cream.

Nutrition Value:

- Calories: 572.1 Cal
- Fat: 41.7 g
- Carbs: 47.8 g

- Protein: 10.5 g
- Fiber: 5.3 g

Chilled Raspberry Soup

Preparation time: 5 minutes
Cooking time: 0 minute
Servings: 2

Ingredients:

- ½ cup cranberry juice cocktail
- 8 cups raspberries and more for topping
- 1 cup coconut sugar
- 2 cups sour cream

Method:

1. Plug in and switch on the NutriBullet blender and then add cocktail, berries and sugar into the jar.
2. Cover with the lid, press 'high', then press 'pulse' and let the ingredients blend until incorporated and smooth.
3. Transfer the mixture into a large bowl, add sour cream and then stir until combined.
4. Cover the bowl with a lid, then refrigerate for a minimum of 2 hours until thoroughly chilled.
5. Garnish soup with more raspberries and then serve.

Nutrition Value:

- Calories: 160 Cal
- Fat: 8 g
- Carbs: 28 g
- Protein: 2 g
- Fiber: 6 g

Banana Fudge Ice Cream

Preparation time: 5 minutes
Cooking time: 0 minute
Servings: 2

Ingredients:

- 2 frozen bananas, sliced
- 6 ounces firm tofu
- 4 tablespoons cocoa powder, unsweetened
- ½ cup peanut butter powder
- 1 teaspoon chocolate chips
- 10 peanuts, chopped

Method:

1. Plug in and switch on the NutriBullet blender and then banana, tofu, cocoa powder and peanut butter powder into the jar.
2. Cover with the lid, press 'high', then press 'pulse' and let the ingredients blend until incorporated and smooth.
3. Divide ice cream between two bowls, top with chocolate chips and peanuts and then serve.

Nutrition Value:

- Calories: 290 Cal
- Fat: 9 g
- Carbs: 46 g
- Protein: 22 g
- Fiber: 12 g

Chapter 5: Condiments and Sauces

Sundried Tomato Marinara Sauce

Preparation time: 5 minutes
Cooking time: 28 minutes
Servings: 4

Ingredients:

- 2 cups vegetable broth
- 1/3 cup sundried tomatoes, packed in oil
- 1 teaspoon sea salt
- 4 cloves of garlic, peeled, roasted, cooled
- 1 tablespoon sugar
- ½ of medium white onion, peeled, roasted, cooled
- 2 tablespoons tomato paste, unsalted
- 1/4 cup basil
- 1 teaspoon Italian seasoning
- 1 teaspoon dried oregano
- 1/4 teaspoon ground black pepper

Method:

1. Plug in and switch on the NutriBullet blender and then add all the ingredients in the order into the jar.
2. Cover with the lid, press 'high', then press 'pulse' and let the ingredients blend until incorporated and smooth.
3. Take a medium pot, place it over medium heat, pour in blended sauce, bring it a simmer and then continue simmering for 25 minutes until reach to desired consistency.
4. When done, remove pot from heat and ladle sauce over cooked pasta.
5. Serve straight away.

Nutrition Value:

- Calories: 46.4 Cal
- Fat: 0.2 g
- Carbs: 10.7 g

- Protein: 1.4 g
- Fiber: 1.3 g

Hummus

Preparation time: 5 minutes
Cooking time: 0 minute
Servings: 32

Ingredients:

- 3 cups canned chickpeas
- 2 cloves of garlic, peeled
- 1/4 cup and 2 teaspoons lemon juice
- 1/4 cup olive oil
- 1/3 cup water
- 1/2 cup tahini
- 1/2 teaspoon sea salt
- 1/4 teaspoon ground cumin

Method:

1. Plug in and switch on the NutriBullet blender and then add all the ingredients in the order into the jar.
2. Cover with the lid, press 'high', and then pulse for 3 to 5 minutes until chickpeas are broken and thick mixture comes together.
3. Tip the hummus into a bowl, sprinkle with red chili powder, drizzle with some more olive oil and then serve.

Nutrition Value:

- Calories: 58.1 Cal
- Fat: 4.1 g
- Carbs: 4.3 g
- Protein: 1.7 g
- Fiber: 1.1 g

Red Salsa

Preparation time: 8 minutes
Cooking time: 0 minute
Servings: 6

Ingredients:

- ½ of medium white onion, peeled, cut into two quarters
- 2 Anaheim pepper, quartered
- 3 cloves of garlic, peeled
- ½ cup cilantro leaves
- 1 teaspoon sea salt
- 1/4 cup dried Chile de Arbol, toasted
- 1 teaspoon sugar
- 2 tablespoons lime juice
- 2 cups diced tomatoes

Method:

1. Plug in and switch on the NutriBullet blender and then add all the ingredients in the order into the jar except for tomatoes.
2. Cover with the lid, press 'high', then press 'pulse' and let the ingredients blend until incorporated and smooth.
3. Add tomatoes, pulse for 3 to 4 minutes until tomatoes break down and mixture has reached to salsa consistency.
4. Tip the salsa into a medium bowl and then serve it with tortilla chips.

Nutrition Value:

- Calories: 39.2 Cal
- Fat: 0.2 g
- Carbs: 6 g
- Protein: 1 g
- Fiber: 2 g

Cranberry and Fig Jam

Preparation time: 5 minutes
Cooking time: 4 minutes
Servings: 20

Ingredients:

- 1 cup orange juice
- 1 cup dry cranberries, sweetened
- 2 tablespoons grated ginger
- 1 cup dried figs, dried
- 1 teaspoon vanilla extract, unsweetened

Method:

1. Take a large heatproof bowl, place all the ingredients in it except for vanilla and then microwave for 4 minutes at high heat setting until ingredients turn soft.
2. Add vanilla, stir until mixed and then transfer the mixture into a jar of NutriBullet blender.
3. Plug in and switch on the blender, cover with the lid, press 'high', then press 'pulse' for four times until all the ingredients have broken.
4. Tip the jam into a bowl and then serve.

Nutrition Value:

- Calories: 50.2 Cal
- Fat: 0.2 g
- Carbs: 13 g
- Protein: 0.4 g
- Fiber: 1.2 g

Guacamole

Preparation time: 5 minutes
Cooking time: 0 minute
Servings: 6

Ingredients:

- ½ of medium red onion, peeled, cut into quarters
- 2 jalapeno peppers, deseeded, quartered
- 3 cloves of garlic, peeled
- ½ cup cilantro leaves
- 1 teaspoon sea salt
- 1 teaspoon ground black pepper
- 2 tablespoons lime juice
- 2 avocado, peeled, pitted, flesh cut into quarters

Method:

1. Plug in and switch on the NutriBullet blender and then add all the ingredients in the order into the jar except for avocado.
2. Cover with the lid, press 'high', then press 'pulse' and let the ingredients blend until incorporated and smooth.
3. Add avocado, pulse for 3 to 4 minutes until avocado break down and thick mixture comes together.
4. Tip the guacamole into a medium bowl and then serve it with tortilla chips.

Nutrition Value:

- Calories: 89.4 Cal
- Fat: 7.4 g
- Carbs: 6.5 g
- Protein: 1.3 g
- Fiber: 3.8 g

Cashew Creamer

Preparation time: 5 minutes

Cooking time: 0 minute

Servings: 128

Ingredients:

- 6 cups of water
- 3 cups cashews, soaked in warm water for 1 hour
- 4 Medjool dates, pitted
- 1/8 teaspoon sea salt
- 1 teaspoon vanilla extract, unsweetened

Method:

1. Plug in and switch on the NutriBullet blender and then add all the ingredients in the order into the jar.
2. Cover with the lid, press 'high', then press 'pulse' and let the ingredients blend until incorporated and smooth.
3. Serve creamer with coffee.

Nutrition Value:

- Calories: 19.9 Cal
- Fat: 1.4 g
- Carbs: 1.5 g
- Protein: 0.6 g
- Fiber: 0.2 g

Pesto

Preparation time: 5 minutes

Cooking time: 0 minute

Servings: 2

Ingredients:

- 1 1/4 cup olive oil
- 3 cups basil leaves
- 1/2 teaspoon sea salt
- 1 ½ cup dried pine nuts, dried
- 1/2 teaspoon ground black pepper
- 8 cloves of garlic
- 2 cups grated parmesan cheese

Method:

1. Plug in and switch on the NutriBullet blender and then add all the ingredients in the order into the jar.
2. Cover with the lid, press 'high' and then pulse for five time for 3 seconds.
3. Then press 'low' button and continue blending the pesto for 30 seconds until smooth.
4. Tip pesto into a bowl and then serve.

Nutrition Value:

- Calories: 236.7 Cal
- Fat: 23.7 g
- Carbs: 3.2 g
- Protein: 4.4 g
- Fiber: 0.5 g

Hollandaise Sauce

Preparation time: 5 minutes
Cooking time: 1 minute
Servings: 6

Ingredients:

- 1/4 teaspoon Dijon mustard
- 1/8 teaspoon Tabasco sauce
- 1 tablespoon lemon juice
- 3 egg yolks
- 1/2 cup butter, unsalted

Method:

1. Plug in and switch on the NutriBullet blender and then add all the ingredients in the order into the jar except for butter.
2. Cover with the lid, press 'high', then press 'pulse' and let the ingredients blend until smooth.
3. Take a medium heatproof bowl, place butter in it and then microwave for 1 minute at high heat setting until it melts and hot.
4. Gradually blend butter into the egg mixture until thick sauce comes together and.
5. Keep sauce warm by placing the jar into a pot containing warm water until ready to serve.

Nutrition Value:

- Calories: 163 Cal
- Fat: 17.5 g
- Carbs: 0.6 g
- Protein: 1.5 g
- Fiber: 0 g

Pistachio Milk

Preparation time: 10 minutes
Cooking time: 0 minute
Servings: 4

Ingredients:

- 1 cup roasted pistachios
- 1 teaspoon vanilla extract. unsweetened
- 4 cups water

Method:

1. Rinse the pistachios.
2. Plug in and switch on the NutriBullet blender, add pistachios into the jar along with vanilla extract and then pour in water.
3. Cover with the lid, press 'high', then press 'pulse' and let the ingredients blend until incorporated and smooth.
4. Take a large jar, cover its mouth with a cheesecloth and then slowly sift the cashew mixture through the cloth.
5. Remove clothe from the jar, and then cool the milk in the jar into the refrigerator for 4 to 6 hours until chilled.
6. Serve straight away.

Nutrition Value:

- Calories: 175.5 Cal
- Fat: 13.1 g
- Carbs: 8.8 g
- Protein: 5.7 g
- Fiber: 3.2 g

BBQ Sauce

Preparation time: 5 minutes
Cooking time: 0 minute
Servings: 30

Ingredients:

- 2 tablespoons honey
- 1 cup ketchup
- 2 tablespoons Worcestershire sauce
- 1/3 cup apple cider vinegar

Method:

1. Plug in and switch on the NutriBullet blender and then add all the ingredients in the order into the jar.
2. Cover with the lid, press 'high', then press 'pulse' and let the ingredients blend until incorporated and smooth.
3. Tip BBQ sauce into a bowl or a jar and then use as desired.

Nutrition Value:

- Calories: 13.7 Cal
- Fat: 0 g
- Carbs: 0 g
- Protein: 0.1 g
- Fiber: 0 g

Conclusion

These recipes are fit for everyone to enjoy Blender dishes beginners and experts in cooking. That is why you need to get this book right now and have easy to make recipes. This will make sure that you always eat homemade meals. With low-carb and low-sugar recipes packed with protein, you and your family can stay healthy by following the keto recipes in the book . Enjoy simple, wholesome food that leave everyone around the table happy and satisfied with The Keto Blendtec Blender Cookbook.

So if you are wondering if the Blender on Keto diet is for you, this is the book that will help you overcome all your concerns and set you on the path to a healthier and stronger you!

Get it now and do yourself a big favor!